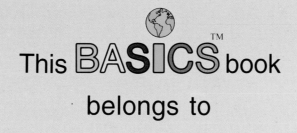

This BASICS book
belongs to

···

···

···

USA

The World

The Galaxy

The Universe

First Aladdin Books edition 1992

Series Editor: Ruth Thomson
Consultants: Ron Mason, England, and William A. Gutsch, Ph.D.,
Hayden Planetarium, American Museum of Natural History, New York

Aladdin Books
Macmillan Publishing Company
866 Third Avenue
New York, NY 10022

Printed in Hong Kong

1 2 3 4 5 6 7 8 9 10

Library of Congress Cataloging–in–Publication Data
Ganeri, Anita. 1961-
And now— the weather / written by Anita Ganeri : illustrated by
Peter Wingham
p. cm.—(Aladdin basics)
Summary: Examines the importance and causes of weather and how it
can change and be predicted.
ISBN 0–689–71583–8
1. Weather—Juvenile literature. [1. Weather.] I. Wingham, Peter, ill.
II. Title. III. Series.
QC981.3.G36 1992
551.6—dc20 91-26682

It might help if you use a globe
when reading this book.
A globe makes it easier to understand
how Earth is tilted and turns.

And now...
the Weather

Written by
Anita Ganeri

Illustrated by

Peter Wingham

Aladdin Books

Macmillan Publishing Company
New York

Maxwell Macmillan International
New York   Oxford   Singapore   Sydney

What is the weather like today?
Is it hot and sunny?
Is it raining?
Is it cold and snowy?
Is it windy?
Is it cloudy and gray?

The weather is important to us.
It affects the way we live,
what we eat, and what we wear.
It even affects the way we feel.

Do any of these pictures look like the weather today?

Without the Sun, nothing could live on Earth.
The Sun makes Earth warm enough
for plants and animals to live on it.

The Sun always stays in the same place.
Earth moves all the time.

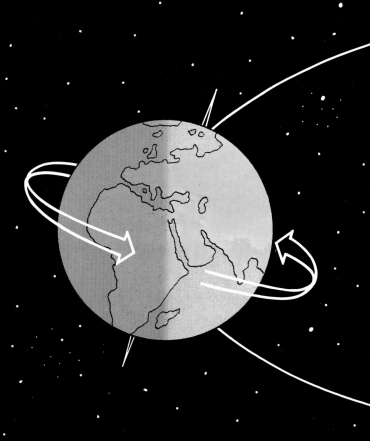

Earth spins in circles.
It takes 24 hours to spin all the way around.
While half of Earth faces toward the Sun,
the other half faces away from it.
This makes day and night.

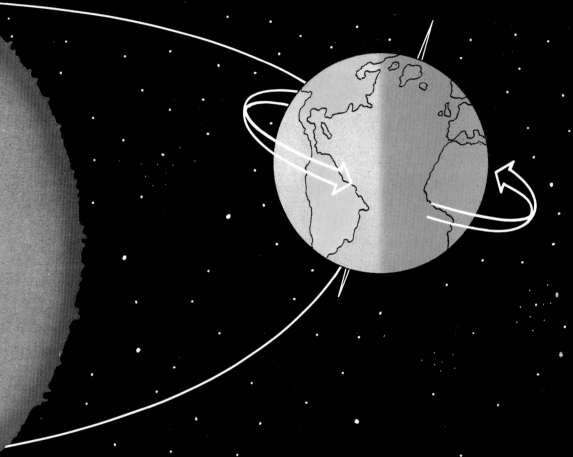

Earth is a lot farther away
from the Sun than it looks here.

Earth also travels around the Sun.
It takes a whole year to go all the way around.
Every time Earth makes a circle around the Sun,
a new year begins.

Earth is tilted. We have drawn a line to show you
how much. Because it is tilted, sometimes a part of it
is close to the Sun, and sometimes it is far away.
When it is close, it has warm weather. This is summer.
When it is far away, it has cold weather. This is winter.

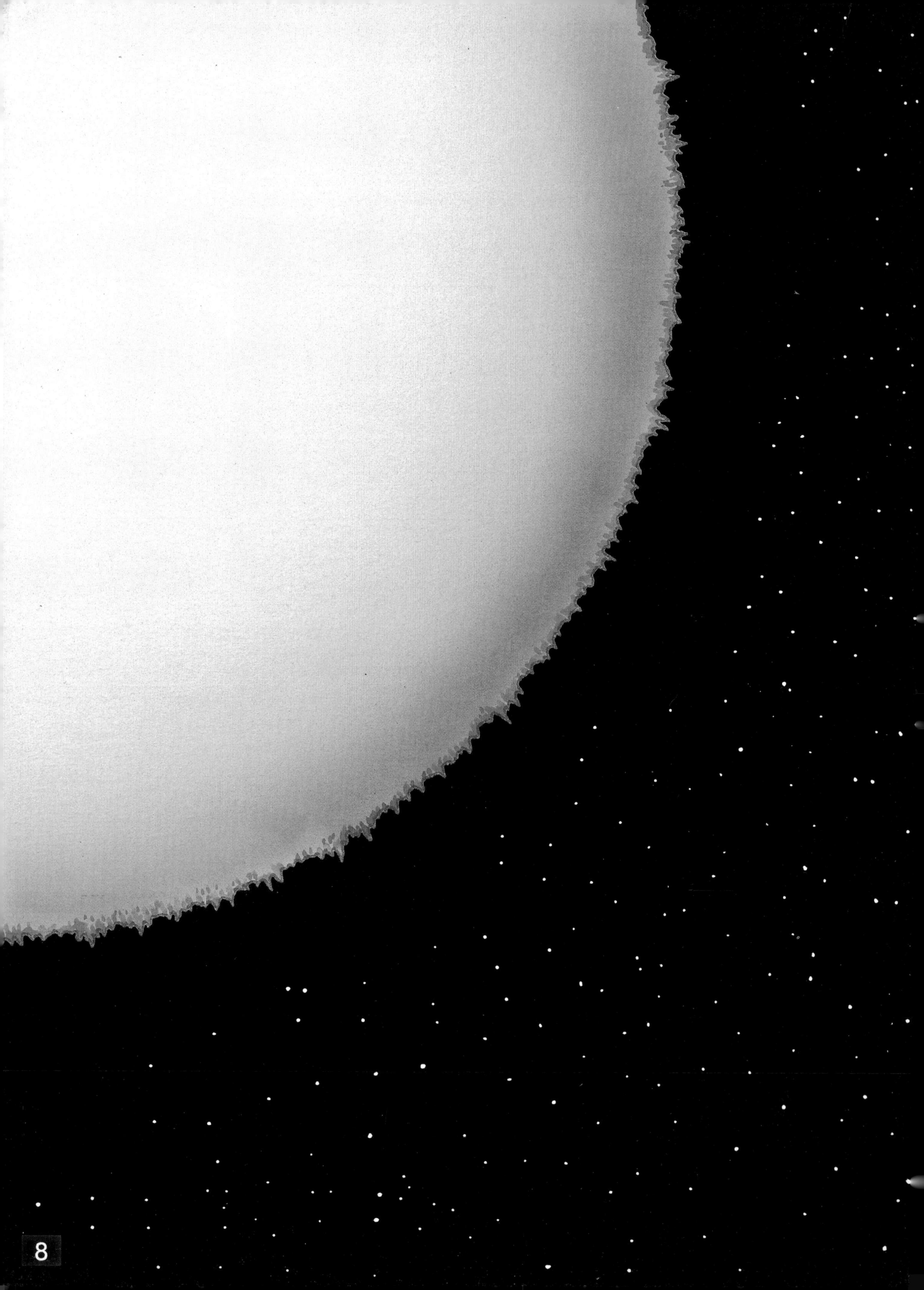

The top and bottom of Earth are called poles.
They are always cold and icy.
The Sun's rays hit these places at an angle,
so its heat isn't very strong.

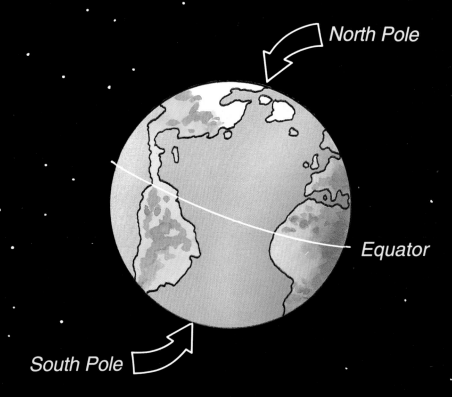

North Pole

Equator

South Pole

The area around the middle of the Earth
is hot all year. This is because
the equator gets lots of direct heat
from the Sun.

Earth is wrapped in an invisible
blanket of air called the atmosphere.
The air in the atmosphere presses
down on Earth. This is called
atmospheric pressure.
There are two kinds of atmospheric
pressure: high and low.

At the equator, the air is warm
and light. Warm air rises,
which makes low pressure.

At the North and South Poles,
the air is cold and heavy.
It presses down hard on Earth,
which makes high pressure.

Air moves from high pressure areas to low pressure areas.
When the warm, light air at the equator rises,
most of the cold air from the poles moves
toward the equator to fill the space.

But the air does not flow in a straight line.
It swirls in different directions as it moves.
This happens because Earth is tilted and spinning.

When air or water moves in one general direction,
it is called a current.
Wind is a current of moving air.
Ocean currents are like huge rivers of water.

Wind and ocean currents help spread
heat from the Sun around Earth.
When the wind blows from a warm place,
it usually carries warm weather with it.
When wind blows from a cold place,
it usually carries some of the cold weather with it.

Some ocean currents are warm, while others are cold.
Each current heats or cools the air above it.
Then the air blows around the world.

The balloon, bird, sailboat, and windsurfer
all use air currents to help them move.

The story of rain

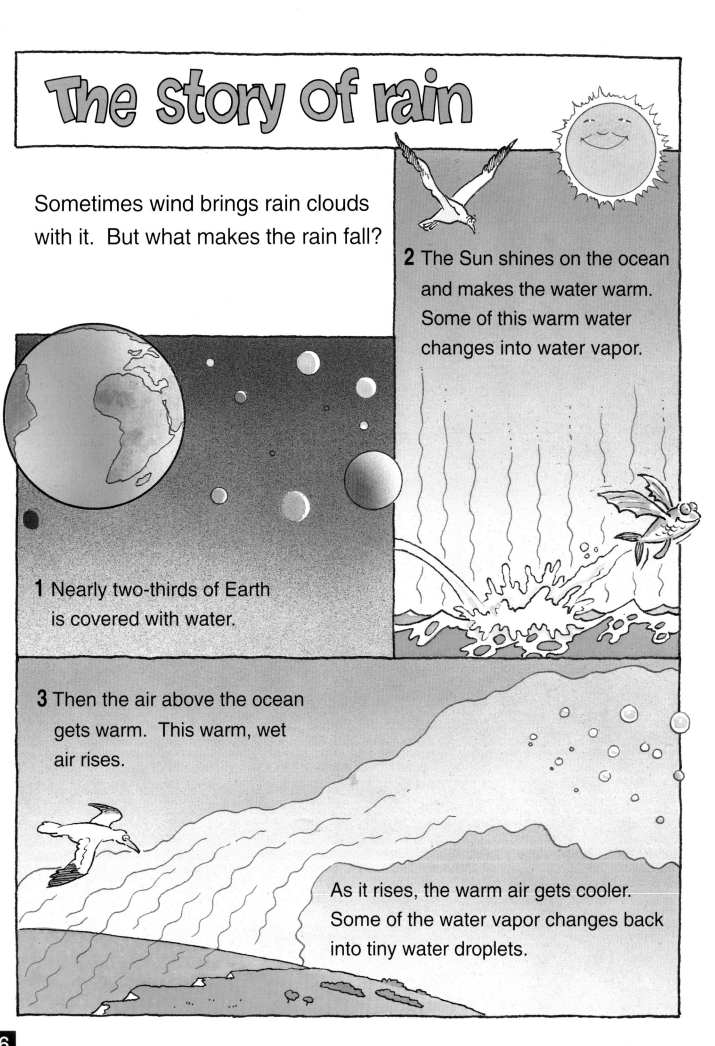

Sometimes wind brings rain clouds with it. But what makes the rain fall?

2 The Sun shines on the ocean and makes the water warm. Some of this warm water changes into water vapor.

1 Nearly two-thirds of Earth is covered with water.

3 Then the air above the ocean gets warm. This warm, wet air rises.

As it rises, the warm air gets cooler. Some of the water vapor changes back into tiny water droplets.

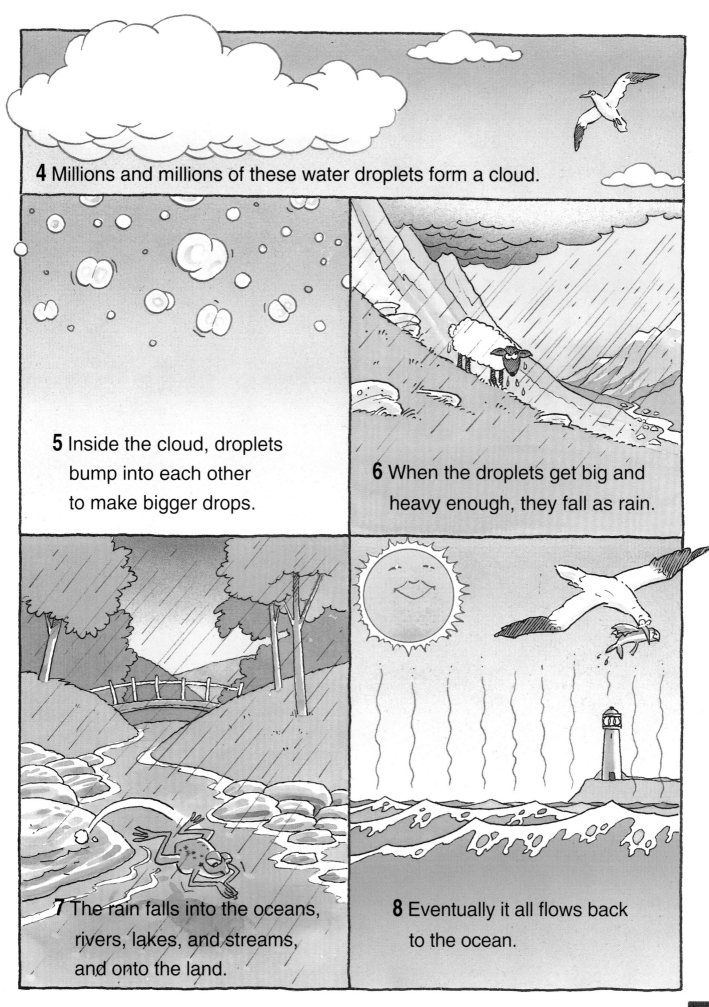

4 Millions and millions of these water droplets form a cloud.

5 Inside the cloud, droplets bump into each other to make bigger drops.

6 When the droplets get big and heavy enough, they fall as rain.

7 The rain falls into the oceans, rivers, lakes, and streams, and onto the land.

8 Eventually it all flows back to the ocean.

When the Sun comes out after a rain shower,
you might see a rainbow in the sky.
As the Sun's light shines through raindrops,
it splits up into colors. The colors of the rainbow
always appear in the same order. Red is at the top,
then orange, yellow, green, blue, indigo
and violet at the bottom.

You can make a rainbow. Stand with your back
to the Sun and use a garden hose to spray
water up into the air. As the Sun shines
through the water, a rainbow will appear.

If you want to see how clouds form, and how rain is made, look at a teakettle when it is boiling. Make sure you stand at a safe distance, though.

As the water inside the teakettle gets hot,
 some of it changes into water vapor.
  When the invisible vapor comes
    through the spout, it meets
    cooler air and changes
   into little clouds of steam.
When a cloud of steam
   touches something
    even cooler,
     like a windowpane,
      the tiny droplets
       of water
        that make up
         the steam
          mix together.
     The droplets
       run down
         the window
          like rain.

Cirrocumulus...
changing weather

Cumulus...
fair weather

20

Cirrus...
rain on the way

There are many different types of cloud.
Different types give us clues
about what the weather will be like.
But the weather can be unpredictable,
and sometimes it doesn't turn out
the way we think it will.

Cumulonimbus...
rain and maybe hail
and thunderstorms

High in the sky, the air is very cold.
When clouds get this high, the water vapor
inside freezes and turns into tiny ice crystals.
The crystals get heavy and fall.
When it is supercold, the crystals don't melt
on their way down. Instead, they stick together
and fall as snowflakes.

If you look at a snowflake through a magnifying glass,
you might see some of these crystals.
Most crystals have six sides.
You will never find two with the exact same pattern.
Next time it snows, catch some snowflakes
and count the different patterns you see.

It's a hot, sticky day.
The sky is full of huge, dark clouds.
Suddenly, a flash of lightning strikes.
Then there is a mighty boom of thunder.

Lightning is a giant spark of electricity.
It flashes from a cloud to the ground
or from cloud to cloud.
It is very, very hot.
As lightning streaks across the sky,
it causes the air around it to expand quickly.
This creates a shock wave in the air,
which makes a booming noise called thunder.

Lightning and thunder happen
at the same time, but you always see
the lightning first. This is because
light travels much, much faster than sound.

Hurricanes and tornadoes are the fiercest storms of all.

Hurricanes are like giant spinning wheels of cloud,
wind, and rain. They usually strike over
warm tropical seas between June and November.

When the air and water vapor above the ocean
get very warm, they rise fast. Sometimes all the heat
makes the air whirl in a circle. It will whirl faster and faster,
and if it whirls fast enough, it will make a hurricane.
Hurricanes churn the sea, making huge waves
that can flood the shore. A hurricane usually dies down
when it moves over cold water or over land.

Tornadoes are long funnels of spinning cloud and wind. They strike over land, usually in spring and summer. During a severe thunderstorm, strong winds can blow in many different directions at once. Sometimes the winds form a giant funnel that hangs down from the thunderstorm cloud. Tornadoes can have winds that blow at 300 miles an hour! Some tornadoes never touch the ground, but when they do, they cause terrible destruction!

Meteorologists are people who study
the weather. Forecasters are people
who tell us what the weather will be like.

Weather forecasts...

...tell farmers if it is a good time
to plant or harvest their crops.

...warn sailors at sea
if a storm is coming.

...let us know if it will rain.
That's useful to know
if you're going out!

...tell us if it is going to snow,
so we can dress warmly.

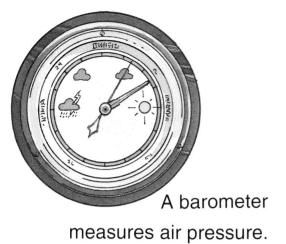

A barometer measures air pressure.

Meteorologists and weather forecasters measure things like the wind, temperature, the amount of water vapor in the air, air pressure, and rainfall. They use these instruments:

A thermometer measures temperature.

A wind sock shows which way the wind is blowing.

A rain gauge measures rainfall.

An anemometer measures wind speed.

INDEX

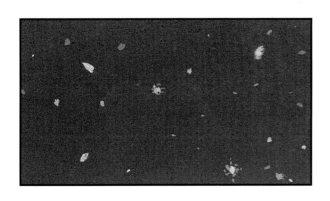

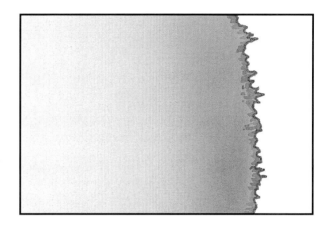

BASICS™

An introduction to our world